### *Excuse me . . .*

"Cold shredded children and se[...]
—from a menu[...]

"Wonderful bargains for men with 16 and [...]
—in a Kentucky clothing store

"Nothing sucks like an Electrolux."
—ad for a Swedish vacuum cleaner

"Visitors are expected to complain at the office between
the hours of 9 and 11am daily."
—in a hotel in Athens

### *. . . and for the ultimate dining experience:*

"Strawberry Crap, Fried Fishermen, Buttered Saucepans, Fried
Hormones, Teppan Yaki—Before Your Cooked Right Eyes, Floating
Iceberg, Organ Chicken"

—from a Japanese menu

From bungled blurbs to dicey directions to screwed-up signs
("Not to be used for the other use"—owner's manual for a food
processor made in Japan), *Free Drinks for Ladies with Nuts* will
have you speaking the language everybody understands:
the language of laughter.

**Jane O'Boyle** is a former publishing executive and the author of
*Wrong! The Biggest Mistakes and Miscalculations Ever Made by
People Who Should Have Known Better* (available from Plume).
She lives in South Carolina.

## ALSO BY JANE O'BOYLE

*Catnip for the Soul*
*Wrong!*

# FREE DRINKS FOR LADIES WITH NUTS

*Delightfully Mangled English from Around the World*

## Jane O'Boyle

A PLUME BOOK

PLUME
Published by the Penguin Group
Penguin Putnam Inc., 375 Hudson Street, New York, New York 10014, U.S.A.
Penguin Books Ltd, 27 Wrights Lane, London W8 5TZ, England
Penguin Books Australia Ltd, Ringwood, Victoria, Australia
Penguin Books Canada Ltd, 10 Alcorn Avenue,
Toronto, Ontario, Canada M4V 3B2
Penguin Books (N.Z.) Ltd, 182–190 Wairau Road, Auckland 10, New Zealand

Penguin Books Ltd, Registered Offices:
Harmondsworth, Middlesex, England

First published by Plume, a member of Penguin Putnam Inc.

First Printing, March, 2000
1  3  5  7  9  10  8  6  4  2

Ⓟ REGISTERED TRADEMARK—MARCA REGISTRADA

LIBRARY OF CONGRESS CATALOGING-IN-PUBLICATION DATA

Free drinks for ladies with nuts : delightfully mangled English from around the
world / [compiled by] Jane O'Boyle.
        p.   cm.
        ISBN 0-452-28114-8
1. English language—Errors of usage—Humor.   2. English language—Foreign
countries—Humor.   3. Communication, International—Humor.
        I. O'Boyle, Jane.
        PN6231.E74 F74 2000
428'.002'07—dc21                                                99-045735

Printed in the United States of America
Set in Americana
Designed by Leonard Telesca

BOOKS ARE AVAILABLE AT QUANTITY DISCOUNTS WHEN USED TO PROMOTE
PRODUCTS OR SERVICES. FOR INFORMATION PLEASE WRITE TO PREMIUM
MARKETING DIVISION, PENGUIN PUTNAM INC.,
375 HUDSON STREET, NEW YORK, NY 10014.

*In memory of Jacques*

*Special thanks to Janis Donnaud,
Clare Ferraro,
and Amanda Patten.*

# CONTENTS

CONTENTS

# FREE DRINKS
# FOR LADIES
# WITH NUTS

# INTRODUCTION

 I've traveled around the world, and have spent much of that time sounding like a fool. While much of this might be attributed to the fact that from time to time I am a fool, some of it derives from the confounding nature of the many languages on this planet. I am careful to watch out for language manholes. However, this does not prevent me from jumping into them on a regular basis, with both feet.

At a country store in Provence, after spotting a delectable jar of red raspberry jam, complete with gingham-covered lid and hand-scrawled label, I smiled and asked the elderly proprietor if I might taste his condoms. He flushed pink and walked away, muttering something under his breath. He looked away in embarrassed silence while I dropped coins in his tray and left the store. He was probably wondering if he could even bring himself to repeat the anecdote later to his lawn-bowling buddies in the park. When you go to France, please bear in mind that "preservatives" are made by Trojan, not by Smuckers. And few people will bother to correct you if you confuse the two, because they are usually too polite to converse with strangers about condoms, in any tongue.

In Istanbul, I told a restaurant waiter that he was a good lamb. He blushed and scurried back to the kitchen. Of course, I'd meant to say I enjoyed my dinner. A couple days later, I saw the waiter in the bazaar—out of uniform—lurking behind a pillar, watching me. Then I found him coming into a mosque just as I was going out. Everywhere I went in Turkey, my lamb was sure to go.

Some say the art of translation lies less in knowing the other language than in knowing your own. Shamed by my trangressions, I built an appreciation for memorable usages of foreign language by people other than me. How can we not admire a person who not only writes something for public inspection, but who boldly states it in a foreign tongue to native speakers? That he or she might make a grammatical error only adds a perfect dash of humility. The true universal language is laughter.

Some of the "lost in translation" citations that swirl around the Internet seem to have originated from a fine book called *Anguished English* by Richard Lederer, which I highly recommend to fans of our skewered language. I am also indebted to my friends and colleagues who were happy to provide their favorite malaprops from ventures abroad. Thanks to them, I have a large collection of cocktail napkins and sticky pamphlets covered in shaky graffiti, as they usually recorded their impressions on the go.

The best part about collecting a lot of mangled English—perhaps we should call it Manglish, a language unto itself—is when you start to think and speak in this dialect yourself. When you speak Manglish, you put yourself in the voice of another, and begin to see the world with new eyeballs. Here is an example of Manglish in a classic movie dialogue. Let's see if you can complete the last line.

HUSBAND: My wife and I are speaking nothing but English now.

WIFE: So we should feel at home when we get to America.

HUSBAND: *Liebchen* . . . sweetest heart, what watch?

WIFE: Ten watch.

HUSBAND: (*frowning*) _____?

Manglish speakers know the last line: "Such much?" If you got this wrong, then not only do you need to read this book, but you also need to watch *Casablanca* a few more times. However, you are not beyond learning what it means for ladies with nuts to get free drinks.

Some people write armchair travel books that reveal the seemingly lost arts of wine making and croissant baking and stone masonry, as might still be found in the rural parts of France or Italy. This book is not the story of European exile, wherein an ugly American becomes a nouvelle artisan, thanks to a kooky neighbor in a beret whose name is GianCarlo. These are the anonymous words of truth and homespun advice from hotel walls and budget restaurants, as observed by typical tourists. These phrases assure us that, even though we may be far from home, we are still among our own kind. Here's a toast to the real people who wrote these words, wherever they are.

# FOR
# YOUR
# INFORMATION

In a Tokyo hotel, in a Munich restaurant, walking down a Hong Kong alley, we are sometimes disarmed by charming messages in English. These signs and public bulletins often carry more meaning than they were intended to have, we observed during our innocent travels abroad.

### *On the grass in a Paris park:*
Please do not be a dog.

### *In a Yugoslavian hotel:*
The flattening of underwear with pleasure is the job of the chambermaid.

### *In a Moscow hotel room:*
The passenger must get free the room before two o'clocks of the day they are abandoning in other case, as the passenger fracture the day and must the administration pay for full.

**Outside a Hong Kong dress shop:**
Ladies have fits upstairs.

**In an Austrian ski resort hotel:**
Not to perambulate the corridor in the hours of
repose in the boots of ascension.

**In a Hong Kong supermarket:**
For your convenience, we recommend courteous
efficient self-service.

**At Osaka airport:**
Shoe sunshine.

### *In a Zurich hotel:*

Because of the impropriety of entertaining guests
of the opposite gender in the bedroom, it is
suggested that the lobby be used for this purpose.

### *In a Mallorca airport:*

Distinguished visitor:

It is known that all the turistic services in Mallorca
are maintaining a correct relation price quality, but
even though, we wish to prize the establishments
and services that to the opinion of our visitors,
surpass notoriously for their quality.

To be able to fill out these questionnaires you must
write the name of this establishment, installation
or turistic service, as is shown below, and you
must give a punctuation between 6 and 10 points
hoping that the service that you must punctuate
has been the best in the relation price-quality.

### *At a restaurant in the Swiss Alps:*
No skies inside.

### *In a Tokyo hotel:*
Is forbitten to steal hotel towels please. If you are not a person to do such a thing is please not to read this notice.

### *In a Nice gift shop:*
Our police: no return, no exchange.

**A sign posted in Germany's Black Forest:**
It is strictly forbidden on our black forest camping
site that people of different gender, for instance
men and women, live together in one tent unless
they are married with each other for that purpose.

**In a Hungarian hotel:**
The lift is bring fixed for the next day. During the
that time we regret that you will be unbearable.

**In a Tokyo ladies' room:**
Tidy HO!

***In a hotel in Athens:***
Visitors are expected to complain at the office
between the hours of 9 and 11am daily.

***At a Bangkok dry cleaner:***
Drop your trousers here for best results.

***At the entrance to a dead-end alley
in Istanbul:***
No more. Please pack up now.

***Outside a Kashmir pension:***
Youth Hostile $10/nite.

***In Hong Kong:***
Nite Club XXX—
DANCING TABLES ALL GIRLS.

***At a Belgrade hotel:***
Restauroom open daily.

***At a Nairobi market:***
Water fountain for humans only.

***Outside an Athens shop:***
PARK ONE HOUR. LATER DICK DOCK GOES
THE MONEY CLOCK.

### *In a Belgrade hotel elevator:*
To move the cabin, push button for wishing
floor. If the cabin should enter more persons,
each one should press a number of the wishing
floor. Driving is then going alphabetically
by national order.

### *In a Milan pension:*
No ladies in the bra—she's lounge only.

### *In a Hong Kong tailor shop:*
Order your summers suit. Because is big rush we
will execute customers in strict rotation.

### In a Mexico bus:
Keep all fours in bus—eyes only out window.

### In a Paris hotel elevator:
Please leave your values at the front desk.

### In a Marrakesh shop:
English smoken.

### On the faucet in a Finnish washroom:
To stop the drip, turn cock to right.

***In a Paris jewelry store:***
Watch guts repaired.

***On an Italian train:***
Water not potatoble.

***In the window of a Swedish furrier:***
Fur coats made for ladies from their own skin.

***At a Hong Kong costume shop:***
For turning tricks on Hallowween.

**At a doctor's office in Rome:**
Specialist in women and other diseases.

**In a German elevator:**
Do not enter lift backwards, and only when lit up.

**In a Normandy museum:**
Brittany, Irland and Whales are almost connected,
and still are today.

**At a museum in Madrid:**
Children Must Enter with Parrots Only.

### In a Rome hotel room:
Please dial 7 to retrieve your auto from the garbage.

### At a Munich museum:
No Photo Pleas.

### In a Tuscan cathedral:
Wake slowly and tssst!

*At an Istanbul hotel pool:*
No Diving.
No Nakedness.
No Ruining.


*At a Barcelona café:*
MISS TOILET LEFT. MISTER TOILET DOWN.

# INTERNATIONAL DELICACIES À LA CARTE

Tasty items, as found on real restaurant menus. When we were daring enough to order these specials, we usually regretted the decision. But we'll leave restaurant reviews to the professionals.

# TODAY'S SPECIALS

## In China

*Cold Shredded Children and Sea Blubber in
Spicy Sauce*

*Fresh Fish Soap*

*Dreaded Veal Cutlet with Potatoes in Cream*

*Barbecue Twin Delights*

*Stir Fried Pine Seeds with Corns*

*Drunken Live Prawns in Chinese Wine*

*Braised Superior Sharksfin Comb with
Seafood & Bamboo Pith Fungus*

*Pustache Ice Cream*

# In Hong Kong

*Indonesian Nazi Goring*

*Fillet Streak, Popotoes and
Chocolate Mouse*

*Wein-weiner*

*Braise of Quayle*

*Egg White with Crab Meat Look*

*Fried Yellow Jack with Eggs and Dough*

*Drunken Pig Leg*

*Individual Cock*

*Streaming Turtle with Sour Beans*

*Famous Drunken Pigeon*

———

"One trip here might not be enough. Sit at one of the many Teppan-Yaki tables to enjoy the exciting knife shows and you'll still have the Japanese, the Thai and the Sushi to try!"

# In Mexico

*Blackened Group with Corn Sauce*

*Sauteed Clawfish*

*Grilled Potties*

# In Egypt

*Muscles of Marines*

*Lobster Thermos*

*Prawn Cock and Tail*

*Lioness Cutlet*

*French Fried Ships*

*Cock in Wine*

*Hot Dog Mustache Pringle*

*Bosom of Chicken*

# In France

*Garlic Coffee*

*Fish Landlady Style*

*Boiled Frogfish*

*Pearts of Artichokes*

*Sweat from the Trolley*

*Chocolate Clam Chowder*

## In South Korea

*Shrimp in a Casket*

*Home-Raised Lionfish*

*Lous Nuts in Syrup*

*Sweet Macapuno Balls*
*(gelatinous mutant coconut)*

## In Nepal

*Fried Friendship*

*Grilled Dachsund*

*Complimentary Glass Wine or Bear*

# In Japan

*Strawberry Crap*

*Fried Fishermen*

*Buttered Saucepans*

*Fried Hormones*

*Teppan Yaki—Before Your Cooked Right Eyes*

*Floating Iceberg*

*Organ Chicken*

## In Vietnam

*Pork with Fresh Garbage*

*Fish Freshly Freed*

*Rice Kooky*

## In Indonesia

*Toes with Butter and Jam*

*Cajun Chicken Biceps*

*Spaghetti Fongoole*

*Loose Fish*

*"Nam Prick" Spicy Thai Sauce Served
with Vegetables Dip*

# In Spain

*Goose Barnacles*

# In Los Angeles

*French Creeps*

*Flank Stake*

*Spaghetti & Neatballs*

*Toe-Shaped Chicken*

*Recent Veal*

*Bagel—Plane or Gallic*

# In Thailand

*Deep-Fried Shrimps Balls*

*Baked Herb Ricce in Pineapple*

*Deep-Fried Sun-Dried Beef*

*Prawn Polls*

# In India

*Macaroni Pappa Zits*

*Cheesecake with Whipped-Flavour Cream*

*Masala Nasti*

---

"Our food will make your eyes water, nostrils sniffle, and tongue reel with the sensational experience."

# In Poland

*Salad a Firm's Own Make*

*Limpid Red Beet Soup with Cheesy
Dumplings in the Form of a Finger*

*Roasted Duck Let Loose*

*Beef Rashers Beaten Up in the Country
People's Fashion*

# MEMORABLE MOVIE SUBTITLES

Actual English subtitles and dubbed dialogue from a selection of foreign films.

*The bullets inside are very hot. Why do I feel so cold?*

□□□

*I got knife scars more than the number of your leg's hair!*

□□□

*I am damn unsatisfied to be killed in this way.*

□□□

*Fatty, you with your thick face have hurt my instep.*

□□□

*I'll fire aimlessly if you don't come out!*

□□□

*Gun wounds again?*

□□□

*Same old rules: no eyes, no groin.*

□□□

*A normal person wouldn't steal pituitaries.*

███████████████

*You always use violence. I should've ordered
glutinous rice chicken.*

□□□

*Damn, I'll burn you into a BBQ chicken!*

□□□

*Beware! Your bones are going to be
disconnected.*

□□□

*Who gave you the nerve to get killed here?*

□□□

*Quiet or I'll blow your throat up.*

□□□

*You daring lousy guy.*

□□□

*Beat him out of recognizable shape!*

□□□

*How can you use my intestines as a gift?*

□□□

*When you're smoking, use the other end!*

███████████████

*Now you see just who is being shown up!*

□□□

*Brand me, will you?*

□□□

*To eat the chicken, first you must catch it with your teeth.*

□□□

*It is a fish style and very effective.*

□□□

*You'll be asking for this!*

□□□

*I'm going to eat you turtles because I hate you all!*

□□□

*I gotta bet you? Ridiculous!*

□□□

*Don't die yet! We're not finished!*

□□□

*Take thy duty.*

*Hey, teacher, what do you think of this piece of meat?*

□□□

*You're not using the secret style?*

□□□

*Your father died trying that style.*

□□□

*Well, my friend, today you're going to die here. Why not just kill yourself?*

□□□

*Glue? What's this glue? You can't glue people!*

□□□

*I call this the cripple style.*
*I call it plain lousy.*

□□□

*If you're going to stick us together, we'll eat dinner upside down.*

□□□

*You are light and sweet, just like soy milk!*

*Whatever you've got, I know it.*

□□□

*We're looking for some guy urgently.*

□□□

*So you feel like touching my arm, do you?*

□□□

*They're coming to kill you, not to kill me.*

□□□

*We'll have the girls first, then we'll all go to the temple later!*

□□□

*Hah! He is only small sweet potatoes.*

□□□

*Get faster than me!*

□□□

*And I'm bigger than you are down there!*

□□□

*We're supposed to be gallanteers, not a couple of poofs with brooms.*

*I don't like being beaten! I'm not like you!*

□□□

*You should get a great deal of brain damage!
Takes one to know one.*

□□□

*They get the male menopores, it makes them
strange!*

□□□

*What are you doing committing suicide in here?*

□□□

*Will you get off? You're squishing my balls.*

□□□

*Twenty years I kept this with me always.*

□□□

*Honey, this food smells weird. Did you fart?*

□□□

*He thought earplugs would save his life.*

□□□

*As the crow flies, so shall you die tonight.*

*There, all your horses are gone. Now teach me to ride!*

□□□

*Look—his torso is here, but his arm is fighting all the way over there!*

□□□

*Don't worry, master, we shall make him a convenient stir fry!*

□□□

# HELPFUL
# INSTRUCTIONS

You don't always have to leave the country to appreciate fine examples of Manglish. These products, purchased at our neighborhood store, came with some practical tips.

*On the packaging for a kitchen knife made*
*in Korea:*
Warning: keep out of children.

*On a box of Christmas lights made*
*in China:*
For indoor or outdoor use only.

*In the owner's manual for a food processor*
*made in Japan:*
Not to be used for the other use.

### *On a Japanese computer software manual:*

Hit mouth two times in rapid succession. Move
mouth so curser will appear on monitor.

### *On a radio made in Germany:*

Very close to translamissing station you may find
useful to put the high low sensitivity to low.

### *On the box of a laughing tip toy made in Vietnam:*

Can't invert with laugh

The laugh begin. you are youthful

Automatize

As poke as shaky as shaky as laugh

During the use. open the lid of top and take two
cells (NO. 5) in the box. If you want to stop laugh
or don't use for a long time. you must take out the
cells (This seller have no cells)

### Excerpts from the instructions on a plastic ice-cube tray, made in China:

The latest style of Instant Non-taste ice-maker

ice of shape Half-circled & flat so that ice dropout
from ice-maker directly that while ice-making &
taking out ice without applying hands to touch ice.
Healthy First!

keep together with other food. without
contaminating with other taste of fishy or
foul-smell. TO be a complete non-taste
& delicious healthy ICE.

Most suitable for cooking picknicking &
recreation applying.

while ice-making finished put whole case in
recreation applying ice-box while outing
for fishing or picknicking it can always keep
long-terms freshing!

There's non-exist color-elements problems that
actually proceed with environmental protections.

***Printed on an eraser made in Japan:***
Mr. Friendly Quality Eraser. Mr. Friendly Arrived!
He always stay near you, and steals in your mind
to lead you to a good situation. We are
ecologically minded. This package will
self-destruct in Mother Earth.

# ADS
# WITH IMPACT

Many foreign companies know the English-speaking market is an important one. Here are some real ads that show expressions above and beyond what we're accustomed to seeing in standard advertising.

### *In a brochure for a French canal cruise:*

What a pleasure to be on the wheel, to feel in control of your holiday!

Free to choose your own route, free to plan your change of scene, free to experience something different. When cruising along the rivers and canals, you will have the peasant impression of setting off for distant horizons.

In France, you can cruise on many canals and see the peculiarities.

***A Buenos Aires newspaper ad for a local
tour company:***

Have you ever imagined yourself canoeing small streams amid a non-stop symphony of insects? Piranha fishing in the slow-flowing waters of one of the most famous rivers in the world? If you ever doubted you could hunt a cayman with your own hands or manufacture your own made-in-the-jungle blowgun, then the Brazilian Amazon is the place to go.

Untouched nature chock o'block with upscale Amazon shopping malls, luxurious jungle-enclosed gated communities next door to the lowest extremes of underdevelopment, five-star boat cruises offering tourists Disneyland-like tribal dances inspired by the remains of the native cultures.

 ## FRENCH CHEESE

France's 400 sorts of cheese could puzzle Mickey Mouse.

The origin of cheese is lost in the mist of time. Thousands of cows and sheeps and goats have been milked since someone first decided to curdle milk. But which sort of cheese shall you choose? According to legislation, cheese means "fermented or not fermented, matured or not matured food, made from diary produce (milk, can be more or less skimmed, or cream or dasher). It can be used as such or coagulated, before it se drained, partly or not. It keeps at least 23% of dry matter."

"The difference between cheese made with pasteurised milk or with milk is a bit ambiguous," Mr. Bersault notices, "some prefer to give no detail about it."

"As a head department, I was dealing with producers directly: this is a token of quality, and a real cheesemonger is able to tell clients when the optimal tasting is over: *the colours of the rinds change: no way to sell then!* I will soon care with the ripening of some sorts myself."

So keep your eye skinned!

How to Choose, to display, to converse and to enjoy cheese . . .

- "Don't lay in amounts of cheese, for it could lose its properties."
- *The tastes of cheese depend on seasons mainly.*
- A cheesemonger will offer you this or that sort because it is splendid: *trust him!*

## FRENCH WINES

Winemaking in France dates back to pre-Roman times, also it was the romans who inseminated the culture of the wine and the practice of winemaking throughout the country. Wine is the product of the juice of fresly picked grapes, after natural or cultural yeasts have converted the grape sugars into alcohol during the fermentation process.

The yeasts, or less, are normally filtered out before bottling.

Each of the ten principal wine producing regions has its own identity, based on grape varieties and terror.

### *A Thai newspaper ad for a souvenir shop:*

We know how to keep our customers happy, by choosing products with eyes, to good looks, good prices and good durability. These factors add up to one less thing for you to wary about on your holiday. Many years of experiments have taught us how to get you. What you want, When you want it. No hassles.

At Pinktree House, our selection gives you the guarantee of quality, so you do not have to replace or repair these souvenirs for a long time. Add to that our restaurant with providing Fresh Seafood & European Cousine is awaiting for you. Also we are just a minute walk to the shooting range & horse riding.

The next time, you're looking for densible souvenirs to take home with you make Pinktree House your first choice, because we guarantee your requirements could save a lot.

### *A Taiwan magazine ad for a*
### *laptop computer:*

Take it to take off away from where other majority
has stayed long since. Not only abreast it keeps
you but also ahead of the cornfield of computing.

### *A travel brochure from the Romanian*
### *region of Prahova:*

Good news! Holiday does not need a certain
season! Winter or summer, spring or autumn,
nature delights you in this gorgeous area. Go back
to nature, the supreme joy of life, and you won't
regret! YOU WON'T REGRET!

Be children again, enjoy the beginnings! Prahova
helps you, being a permanent surprise. Come
now! COME NOW!

Holiday is here. Now you can do anything or even more. WHY NOT?

Joy, colour, genuine customs. Folklore is the expression of authentic life. IT IS!

Unforgettable nights—close to the stars, scent of hay, fairy tales: the spell is cast on you. LOVE!

In the long string of surprises offered by the Prahova Valley, Sinaia gleams promisingly. The air breaths the memory of great people, leaving enough room to your soul eager for life and fun. FUN!

### *From a magazine ad for a translation company in France:*

In order to guarantee the homogeneity and quality of the translated text, we consider that terminology is the major deal, the obliged passage. We are relying on our basic terminological data of the concerned area and taking into account the specific terminology of the company involved after she has validated it.

Besides, the computer toolls we use allow us to enrich continously customer's terminology all along the cooperation process between him and us.

Passing the source text through the lemmatiser allows the lexical analysis which creates the list of missing terms. The appropriate vocabulary being available in the system, it makes out a gross translation, technically correct.

### *A tour guide to Rio de Janiero:*

A couple discos in Rio are "privates clubs," meaning you have to have a member or be a guest of an expensive hotel to get in (Rhinoceros like this). Most have an open-doors policy, though, and welcome everybody.

The night gets hotter after 12 midnight. Before that most Cariocas are at friend's houses or at bars, warming up to stretch the evening. Beware!

### *In a Moscow tour guide:*

One of the longest bars in Moscow meets you in the "Snowstorm" nightclub a floor above where over 800 sq. m. are at your disposal for tet-a-tet dinner or weird dancing on the cherry stained floor while posh ladies in vivid dresses and immaculate men will be a pleasant view for your eyes. Wait till after midnight the life show will start with hot pop star invited to perform.

A friendly but effective metal detector as well as some other devices are going to ensure that you are safe and sound while you go through all the excitements of the night.

# HELPFUL INSTRUCTIONS IN YOUR NATIVE TONGUE

They may be able to use English correctly, but sometimes product manufacturers play a little Manglish of the mind. We suspect that some of these package instructions were implemented by corporate legal departments. Just to be mischievous, we sometimes disobey the instructions, but we do not recommend you do the same.

***Printed on a bag of Fritos:***
You could be a winner! No purchase necessary.
Details inside.

***On the wrapper of a bar of Dial soap:***
Directions: Use like regular soap.

***On a frozen dinner:***
Serving suggestion: Defrost.

***A box containing a hotel shower cap:***
Fits one head.

***On the bottom of the package for a
tiramisu dessert:***
Do not turn upside down.

***Consumer advisory on a package of English
bread pudding:***
Product will be hot after heating.

***A bottle of children's cough medicine:***
Do not drive car or operate machinery.

***In a package of sleeping pills:***
Warning: may cause drowsiness.

### On a chain-saw manual:
Do not attempt to stop chain with your hands.


### On a little bag of airline peanuts:
Instructions: open packet, eat nuts.


### On a full-sized package of peanuts:
Warning: contains nuts.


### On a hair dryer:
Do not use while sleeping.

# HALF-SLIPS
# OF THE
# TONGUE

Sometimes people who speak English get so used to it, they don't always pay attention.

***Sign at an American military base:***
Restricted to unauthorized personnel.

***At a California restaurant:***
Open 365 days a year (closed on Thanksgiving).

***At a New York nursing home:***
For the sick and tired of the Episcopal Church.

***A Minnesota shopping mall marquee:***
—Archery Tournament
—Ears Pierced

**At a Detroit savings and loan:**
Ask about our plans for owning your home.

**In a Miami hospital maternity ward:**
No children allowed.

**In a Kentucky clothing store:**
Wonderful bargains for men with 16
and 17 necks.

**At a Santa Fe gas station:**
We will sell gasoline to anyone in a
glass container.

### In New York City:
MARITAL ARTS STUDIO

### At an Ohio shop:
We buy junk and sell antiques.

### In a Pennsylvania cemetery:
Persons are prohibited from picking flowers from any but their own graves.

### In a California church bulletin:
Thursday night—Potluck supper. Prayer and medication to follow.

**Sign on a New York City clothing shop:**
Second floor. Upstairs.

**In a New York newspaper ad:**
Read a book in 15 minutes!
Haven't you always wanted a photogenic
memory?

**In a South Carolina church bulletin:**
The service will close with "Little Drops of Water."
One of the ladies will start quietly and the rest of
the congregation will join in.

# BRAND NAMES WE REMEMBER

Some companies have entire departments dedicated to the naming of new products. Words that sound perfect rolling off the tongue, however, are not always appropriate in other languages. When Starbucks coffee shops created a tea beverage called "tiazzi," for example, they chose a name that means "my ass" in certain Arabic dialects. In the 1920s, Coca-Cola launched in China with a name that translated to "Bite the wax tadpole."

Here are some products with unusual English names that we found in shops around the globe.

# CHINA

**Clean Finger Nail**
tissues

**Ass Glue**
glue

**Swine**
chocolate

**Libido**
soda

**Homo**
fish sausage

**Coloured Prawn**
crackers

**Double Apricots Brand**
canned cabbage

**Love Letters**
coffee-flavor egg roll cookies

## THAILAND

**Parrot Toilet**
soap

**Temple of Heaven**
green tea Special Gunpowder

## INDIA

**Ban Cock**
bug repellent

**Purge**
detergent

## GERMANY

**Hornyphon**
video recorder

**Assman**
tape recorder

# JAPAN

**Kolic**
mineral water

**Creap Creamy Powder**
coffee creamer

**Last Climax**
tissue

**Pocari Sweat**
eye-opener sports beverage

**Shocking**
chewing gum

**Cat Wetty**
moistened hand towels

**Beverages Relax**
coffee

**Dydo**
coffee

**Jive**
coffee

**It's On My Mind**
tea-flavored soda

**Don't!**
how-to magazine for boys

**Croissant**
home magazine for women

**SomeTime Fresh**
cigarettes

**Chocolate Colon**
cookies

**No Time**
gum

**Snacks Pickle Ex**
bourbon-flavored chocolates

**Fresh Time Shower**
candy

**Pocky**
crème brûlée

**Hot-Kid**
coconut jelly

**Slicky**
deodorant

**Naïve**
cream rinse

**Sport Balls**
coconut candy

## FRANCE

**Loafer**
bus company

**Gag**
bottled beverage

**Donkey Train**
soap

## MALAYSIA

**Foco Pennywort**
soda pop

**Telephone**
agar-agar powder

**Luxury**
crackers

**Battleship**
canned squid

# MEMORABLE ADVERTISING SLOGANS

They speak for themselves.

## IN JAPAN

### For Snickers candy bars:
"Get!"

### Cream soda products:
"Too fast to live, too young to happy."

### For Cabin cigarettes:
"Today I Smoke, Today I Smoke Today I Smoke, Yes."

### For gummy candy:
"Its translucent color so alluring and taste and aroma so gentle and mellow offer admiring feelings of a graceful lady. Enjoy soft and juicy Muscat gummy."

***For KissMint chewing gum:***
"55% less calories than average gums. Not only delicious but also contains various effective ingredients."

***On Coca-Cola cans:***
"I FEEL COKE AND SOUND SPECIAL."

***A major ad slogan for a new web browser starred the cartoon character Woody Woodpecker, although the campaign was cancelled the day before its multimillion-dollar global launch:***
"Touch Woody—The Internet Pecker"

***For UCC "Drink It Black" coffee:***
"Black coffee has great features which other coffees have never had: non-sugar."

## IN ENGLAND

"Orange juice. It gets your pecker up."

**Ad for a Tanganyika animal reserve:**
"See elephants, lions and cheaters!"

**Ad for a Canary Islands cruise:**
"Don't take a vacation . . . Have a Love Affair . . .
$900 all inclusive."

_____

**Advertisement for donkey rides in Thailand:**
"Would you like to ride on your own ass?"

**For a Chinese soup:**
"No antiseptics and artificial pigments!"

### *Ad for a Swedish vacuum cleaner:*
"Nothing sucks like an Electrolux."

### *For a Hong Kong dentist:*
"Teeth extracted by the latest Methodists."

# AND NOW, THE NEWS . . .

Reading English-language newspapers in foreign countries can help you feel more at home. And yet there is always a foreign flair.

*From the Air Azores in-flight magazine:*

# Woodcraving

It is one of the most intensely cultivated forms of art in the city. In woodcraving, the treatment of the intense plasticism converges with the condensement of the notion of volume developed by the artisans, imprinting an irresistable dynamic that submits the statuary, predominating the despotism of framing and the luxurious beauty of ornamentation.

*From a Ghanian newspaper:*

# Hundreds Pay Last Respect to Late Dormaa Queenmother

People from all walks of life thronged the Palace at Dormaa yesterday to pay their last respects to the late queenmother, Nana Owusu Oduro, a royal of the Dormaa stool, who died in February at age 54. Ministers, members of parliament, district chief executives and chiefs were among the mourners who fled past the body. Nana Owusu Oduro, who was enstooled queenmother in 1977, is survived by eight children.

# Ban Body Odour

Nothing can be more embracing than bad body odour. And the problem only gets worse summers. With the kind of care products available today there should be little excuse for odour.

But there is nothing worse than a highly perfumed deodourant overlaying the smell of sweat. Bad body odour can be caused by a number of factors like improper hygiense, synthetic fabrics, tight fitting clothes, overindulgence in highly spiced and flavoured foods, as well as prolonged medication.

## Body odour dispellers

There are several home remedies to make you smell clean and healthy.

- Fresh green cocktail: Place a good selection of green vegetables like cucumbers, carrots green leafy vegetables with addition of tomatoes, seasoning, lemon and a little water into a blender. Dilute if necessary. These green vegetables of chlorophyll which dispels bad odours and gases and also have a laxative effect, in system.

- Dandy deodourants: Market deodourants contain an aluminium compound which is not advisable to be used frequently. Use it when there is absolutely no time for a quick bath. Antiperspirants are not advisable since they block the sweat glands, which become a hub of skin infection, allergies and itching.

### *From Budapest:*

*Madonna was in Hungary filming the movie*
Evita *when she was intervewed by the Budapest
newspaper* Blikk. *The questions were asked in
Hungarian, then translated into English for her;
her replies were then translated back into
Hungarian. Legend has it that* USA Today
*wanted a copy of it. So the* Blikk *interview was
retranslated from Hungarian back into English.
This is the result:*

BLIKK: Madonna, Budapest says hello with arms
that are spread-eagled. Did you have a visit here
that was agreeable? Are you in good odor? You
are the biggest fan of our young people who
hear your musical productions and like to move
their bodies in response.

MADONNA: Thank you for saying these compli-
ments {*holds up hands*}. Please stop with taking
sensationalist photographs until I have removed
my garments for all to see. This is a joke I
have made.

BLIKK: Madonna, let's cut toward the hunt: are you a bold hussy-woman that feasts on men who are tops?

MADONNA: Yes, yes, this is certainly something that brings to the surface my longings. In America it is not considered to be mentally ill when a woman advances on her prey in a discotheque setting with hardy cocktails present. And there is a more normal attitude toward leather play-toys that also makes my day.

BLIKK: Is this how you met Carlos, your love-servant who is reputed? Did you know he was heaven-sent right off the stick? Or were you dating many other people in your bed at the same time?

MADONNA: No, he was the only one I was dating in my bed then, so it is a scientific fact that the baby was made in my womb using him. But as regards those questions, enough! I am a woman and not a test-mouse! Carlos is an everyday person who is in the orbit of a star who is being muscled-trained by him, not a sex machine.

BLIKK: May we talk about your other "baby," your movie then? Please do not be denying that the similarities between you and the real Evita are grounded in basis. Power, money, tasty food, Grammys—all these elements are afoot.

MADONNA: What is up in the air with you? Evita never was winning a Grammy!

BLIKK: Perhaps not. But as to your film, in trying to bring your reputation along a rocky road, can you make people forget the bad explosions of "Who's That Girl?" and "Shanghai Surprise?"

MADONNA: I am a tip-top starlet. That is my job that I am paid to do.

BLIKK: OK, here's a question from left space. What was your book "Slut" about?

MADONNA: It was called "Sex," my book.

BLIKK: Not in Hungary. Here it was called "Slut." How did it come to publish. Were you love-making with a man-about-town printer? Do you prefer making suggestive literature to fast-selling CDs?

MADONNA: There are different facets to my career highway. I am preferring only to become respected all over the map as a 100% artist.

BLIKK: There is much interest in you from this geographic region, so I must ask this final questions: How many Hungarian men have you dated in bed? Are they No. 1? How are they comparing to Argentine men, who are famous being tip-top as well?

MADONNA: Well, to avoid aggravating global tension, I would say it's a tie (*laugh*). No, no. I am serious now. See here, I am working like a canine all the way around the clock! I have been too busy to try the goulash that makes your country one for the record books.

BLIKK: Thank you for the candid chitchat.

MADONNA: No problem, friend who is a girl.

# FRACTURED MOVIE MARQUEES

The beauty of changeable letter signs is that you can attract potential movie audiences. In fact, you might draw even larger crowds if you are missing a few letters. Here are movies we have seen posted at theaters.

**EAR OF LIVING
DANGEROUSLY**

**SHAK IN LOVE**

**HANNAH AND
HER SISTS**

BUGS LI E

TURN OF JED

TIT NIC

**CASHBLANCA**

**TAXI RIVER**

**BRAVE ART**

RAIN MAN ACCUSED

SHIN

SCENT OF OMAN

U FORGIVEN

HOWARDS UNFORGIVEN

MONSTRUCK

SHINDLER LIT

AM IN PARIS

LEGS OF FALL

DEAD MAN
WALKING LAS VEGAS

FOR GUM

DANCES WITH LAMBS

# AND
# FURTHERMORE

Signs and public notices observed on subsequent trips abroad.

**At a Paris airport customs office:**
Animals under three months old are not allowed
in France.

**Outside a Hong Kong tavern:**
GIRLS GIRLS GIRLS—Live Shoes Daily.

**In a Bangkok temple:**
It is forbidden to enter a womman even a
foreigner if dressed as a man.

**On the wall of a bank in Ghana:**
DO NOT URINATE HERE FINE SPOT 2000.

### In a Hong Kong bar:
Free drinks for ladies with nuts.

### Detour sign in Kyushi, Japan:
Stop: Drive Sideways.

### At the Budapest Zoo:
Please do not feed the animals. If you have any
suitable food, give it to the guard on duty.

***In the lobby of a Moscow hotel, across from
a Russian Orthodox monastery:***
You are welcome to visit the cemetery where
famous Russian and Soviet composers, artists and
writers are buried daily except Thursday.

***On a radiator in an Edinburgh bed
and breakfast:***
For overnight warmth, use a lot of P.

***In a Norwegian cocktail lounge:***
Ladies are suggested not to have children in
the bar.

### *In a Paris guidebook:*

To call a broad from France, first dial 00, then the
country's code and then your number.

### *On the menu of a Swiss restaurant:*
Our wines leave you nothing to hope for.

### In a four-star hotel room in the South of France:

Your attention please. First. It is absolutely forbidden take the cover and the counterpane to go in the garden for take sun. Secondly, it's absolutely forbid to go out by windows because all curtains are damaged. Third, you are request take care when you take shower because innondation rot the carpet. But after this instructions, you don't take care, I'll be obliged to take sanctions. The direction.

### In a Tokyo rental car:

When passenger of foot heave in sight, tootle the horn. Trumpet him melodiously at first, but if he still obstacles your passage then tootle him with vigor.

***In a Hong Kong shoe store:***
Cinderella shoe—in all sighs!

***In a Swiss hotel:***
Special today—no ice cream.

***A foreign company chairman, upon ending
a late meeting with his American associates:***
"Early to bed and up with the cock!"

***At a Paris discount store:***
Marzipan in-shape Jesus, 6 francs.

### *In an Acapulco hotel:*

The manager has personally passed all the water served here.

### *At a Hong Kong florist:*

Beautiful arrangements for your Wetting Event!

### *In a St. Tropez hotel room:*

Shoulder desires you room service, press 7.

### *In an Arles public phone booth:*
Warning All Telephoners:
If you use this telephone without a cart, you will
be emprisoned.

### *In a Chinese fortune cookie:*
This is only a fortune cookie fun thing, generated
at radon by the computer. We are not libel for any
loss or damage caused by or arising from the use
of the information herein.

### *At a Seoul hotel desk:*
Choose twin bed or marriage size; we regret no
King Kong size.

*A professional translator during
a meeting at the Vatican:*
"And now, his poopiness the Hole . . . er . . .
His poopiness the Pole . . . rather, His Holiness
the Poop."

*At a Singapore restaurant:*
Eat in or Take Off.

*On a Greek fishing pier:*
No hooking.

*On a Mediterranean cruise ship:*
DO NOT LEAN ON THE WIDOW.

**At the Paris Trocadero monument:**
Attention Tumbling.

**At a Calcutta hotel desk:**
Weather Today—Sun or Rain.

**At a French cafeteria:**
Service Self—First Take Plate Form Here.

**At a Turin pension:**
We are not responsive to your valuable losses
unless they are in hotel safe.

***At a Mexico City hotel:***
MAD SERVICE DAILY 8 TO 12.


***On a Marseilles hotel doorknob tag:***
PRIVY PLEASE

***At a Brunei hotel:***
Keep shutters close or monkey make you crazy.

We are always on the lookout for new signs, package instructions and menu items that are unique and eye-refreshing. Please send us any items so we can catalog them—and credit you!

Send pleasing copies (for no return sorry) to:

LADIES WITH NUTS
c/o Plume Books
Penguin Putnam Inc.
375 Hudson Street
New York, NY 10014

 **PLUME**

---

## ALSO OF INTEREST

**WRONG!** *The Biggest Mistakes and Miscalculations Ever Made by People Who Should Have Known Better*—**Jane O'Boyle** "The Internet will collapse within a year."—Bob Metcalf *Wrong!* contains the finest in faux pas from the world's most famous masters of miscalculation, sultans of shortsightedness, and Einsteins of error.

0-452-28112-1

**SAY ANYTHING** *The Movie Quote Game That Takes You Back to the '80s se Line at a Time*—**Peter J. Fornatale and Frank R. Scatoni** What's the greatest period in movie history? The '80s, of course. If you got that right, trade in the ripped sweatshirt and leg warmers for the funniest, most outrageous movie game that takes players straight back to the '80s.

0-452-28147-4

**SIX DEGREES OF KEVIN BACON**—**Craig Fass, Brian Turtle, and Mike Ginelli** In dorms, in offices, on the Internet, and across the nation, everyone's connecting everyone to Kevin Bacon. Welcome to *Six Degrees of Kevin Bacon,* where everything revolves around one man, and one man alone.

0-452-27844-9

---

# ℗ PLUME

---

**STRANGE TAILS** *All-Too-True News from the Animal Kingdom*—**John J. Kohut and Roland Sweet** From primates running in primaries to drunk and disorderly donkeys; from fowl play to feline fetishes; from birdbrains to the furry folk who make monkeys out of all of us, after reading the true stories told in *Strange Tails* you'll never look at your pets the same way again.

0-452-28118-0

**REAL SEX** *Titillating but True Tales of Bizarre Fetishes, Strange Compulsions, and Just Plain Weird Stuff*—**John J. Kohut and Roland Sweet** An all new compilation of true stories exposing the sexual fetishes, predilections, and mishaps of the deviant majority.

0-452-28151-2

---

**ⓟ  PLUME**

---

**DUMB, DUMBER, DUMBEST** *True News of the World's Least Competent People*—**John J. Kohut & Roland Sweet**  Compiled from legitimate news sources around the world, this uproarious book is a guided tour through the hilarious halls of buffoonery and incompetence, telling more than five hundred true stories of unsurpassed stupidity.

0-452-27595-4

**MORE DUMB, DUMBER, DUMBEST** *True News of the World's Least Competent People*—**John J. Kohut & Roland Sweet**  From moronic marriages, outlandish deaths, half-witted crimes, and implausible lawsuits to dull-witted criminals, lunatic lovers, and simpleminded spouses, these certifiably stupid real-life stunts comprise a comprehensive compendium of cluelessness.

0-452-27891-0

---